Mum...

A TREASURY OF WIT, INSULTS AND FIGHT-STARTERS

Crombie Jardine
PUBLISHING LIMITED
Office 2, 3 Edgar Buildings
George Street
Bath
BA1 2FJ
www.crombiejardine.com

Published by Crombie Jardine Publishing Limited
First edition, 2007

Copyright © Chris Pilbeam 2007

All rights are reserved. No part of this publication may be reproduced, stored in a retrieval system, or transmitted, in any form or by any means, electronic, mechanical, photocopying, recording or otherwise, without the prior written permission of the publisher.

10-digit ISBN 1-905102-71-2
13-digit ISBN 978-1-905102-71-6

Written by Chris Pilbeam
Designed by www.glensaville.com
Printed and bound in Great Britain by
William Clowes Ltd, Beccles, Suffolk

INTRODUCTION

Jake was a giant of a man with a violent reputation. A quick-tempered amateur boxer and street brawler, he worked as a bouncer in one of the South Coast's roughest pubs where he dispensed summary justice to rowdy locals and drunken sailors. One night, Jake was standing at

the bar when a thin, scruffy old man barged his way through the crowd, clearly the worse for drink. The old man raised a grubby hand and pointed straight at Jake.

"I did it with your mum," the old man yelled, "and she was absolutely filthy."

Silence fell over the pub and all

eyes turned to the bar. A couple of muscles in Jake's huge neck began to twitch. The crowd moved away nervously, leaving only Jake and the old man standing there.

"I did it with your mum, mate," the old man sang, poking Jake in the chest. "And she loved it. She was screaming for more. What do you think of that, sonny?"

"Go home, dad," said Jake.
"You're drunk."

Poor Jake. It's a rule of life that no one likes to hear bad things about their mum.

The only time it's excusable is when it's done with style.

In America, long before the days of

Eminem and hip-hop battles, there was a game of wits known as 'the dozens'. Two opponents would face each other in front of a crowd and trade quick-fire insults until one of them lost their temper.

The quickest way of winning wasn't to pick on your opponent - it was to go for the jugular and pick on your opponent's mum. From this

game, the 'Your Mum' one-liner was born. Childish, mean and funny, these jokes were tailored to raise an opponent's blood pressure while keeping the crowd in stitches.

This is the definitive collection of Your Mum jokes. They're not for all occasions. A riot squad was called to a London school fairly recently to deal with a mass brawl. Once

the dust had settled, it turned out that the whole thing had started over an ill advised Your Mum joke. It sometimes pays to keep these to yourself, it seems.

Mum's the word, folks.

Chris Pilbeam
2007

Your mum's so ugly that when she walks past the bathroom the toilet flushes.

Your mum's so fat she went to the zoo and an elephant threw her a peanut.

Your mum's so ugly that when she looks in the mirror, the reflection shakes its head.

Your mum's so poor that when I ring the doorbell she says, 'ding'.

Your mum's so old she took her driving test in a chariot.

Your mum's so fat that when your dad got on top of her, he burnt himself on the light bulb.

Your mum's so fat that weather forecasters assign names to her farts.

Your mum's so stupid she lost a finger and now she can't count past nine.

Your mum's so fat she fell over and rocked herself asleep trying to get up again.

Your mum's so poor she does drive-by shootings on the bus.

Your mum's so hairy she shaved her back and lost a stone.

Your mum's breath is so bad that I called her on the phone and got an ear infection.

Your mum's so ugly the psychiatrist makes her lie face down.

Your mum's so fat she fell in love and broke it.

Your mum's so fat her cereal bowl came with a lifeguard.

Your mum's so stupid her idea of safe sex is locking the car doors.

Your mum's so poor that when I asked her what was for dinner, she put her foot on the table and said 'corn'.

Your mum's like the sun: if you stare at her too long you go blind.

Your mum's like a doorknob: everyone gets a turn.

Your mum's so fat
that when she goes to the cinema they project the film on her back.

Your mum's so fat
that people jog around her for exercise.

Your mum's so old she farts dust.

Your mum's so fat she sets off car alarms when she walks.

Your mum's so ugly she went into a haunted house and came out with a job offer.

Your mum's so fat she stood in front of the Hollywood sign and it just said H D.

Your mum's so stupid she got locked in a grocery store and starved.

Your mum's so stupid
she got locked in the bathroom and wet herself.

Your mum's so poor
people break into her house and leave money.

Your mum's so fat they used her for a trampoline at the Olympics.

Your mum's so dirty that I stuck a cotton bud in her ear and pulled out a candle.

Your mum's so ugly the doctor slapped himself when she was born.

Your mum's so old she walked into an antique auction and three people bid on her.

Your mum's so fat you have to grease your front door and put a biscuit on the other side just to get her through.

Your mum's so fat her picture broke the wall.

Your mum's so fat she was born with a silver shovel in her mouth.

Your mum's so short she can do back flips under her bed.

Your mum's so stupid she thinks a two-income family is where your dad has two jobs.

Your mum's so old she gets nostalgic when she reads the Bible.

Your mum's so thin she has to run around in the shower to get wet.

Your mum's so stupid she failed a survey.

Your mum's so fat that after the divorce, all she took was the food.

Your mum's so fat she has to wear a sock on each toe.

Your mum's so poor that I saw her walking down the street with one shoe on. I asked her if she'd lost a shoe and she said, 'no – just found one'.

Your mum's so ugly they pay her to put her clothes on in strip clubs.

Your mum's breath is so bad that when she yawns, her teeth duck.

Your mum's so fat she uses a playground slide for a shoehorn.

Your mum's so fat she sat on a five-pound note and tears came out of the Queen's eyes.

Your mum's so stupid she got hit by a parked car.

Your mum's so stupid she put out the cigarette butt that was heating your house.

Your mum's so fat
she has to put on her belt with
a boomerang.

Your mum's so poor
she can't even afford to
pay attention.

Your mum's so fat she has
to get out of bed in sections.

Your mum's so fat she smells like bacon on hot days.

Your mum's so fat when her phone goes off, people think she's reversing.

Your mum's birth-sign: 'Red Light District'.

Your mum's so old that when she was at school, there was no history class.

Your mum's like Chinese food: sweet, sour and cheap.

Your mum's so thin she only has one stripe on her pyjamas.

Your mum's so ugly she went for a sex change and the doctor had to flip a coin.

Your mum's so ugly she scares blind children.

Your mum's teeth are so yellow that traffic slows down when she smiles.

Your mum's so fat she roller-skates on two buses.

Your mum's so poor that when she invited me for dinner, I picked up a paper plate and she shouted at me for using the good china.

Your mum's so ugly that when they took her to the beautician, it took 12 hours for a quote.

Your mum has so much dandruff her head lice have to wear snowshoes.

Your mum's so fat she uses pillowcases for socks.

Your mum's so fat they have to grease the bathtub to get her out.

Your mum's so old she got slapped by Eve for flirting with Adam.

Your mum's so fat her blood type is ketchup.

Your mum's so stupid that when someone told her to take out the rubbish, she put your dad in the garden.

Your mum's so fat her shoes smile when she takes them off.

Your mum's so old her memory is in black and white.

Your mum's so stupid she sits on the TV and watches the sofa.

Your mum's house is so dirty that people wipe their feet before going outside.

Your mum's like a beautiful tropical beach: she has crabs.

Your mum's so fat she has to keep pound coins in one pocket and Chinese money in the other.

Your mum's so fat she snorts lines of ham.

Your mum's so ugly she got arrested for vandalising a mirror shop.

Your mum's so ugly I thought she was your dad.

Your mum's so hairy that when you were born, you almost died of carpet burn.

Your mum's so fat that when she goes to the fair, kids try to ride her.

Your mum's so fat that when she went bungee jumping she took the bridge with her.

Your mum's so stupid she took an IQ test and it came back negative.

Your mum's so stupid
she saw a sign saying 'wet floor' so she did.

Your mum's house is so small
that when she orders a large pizza, she has to go outside to eat it.

Your mum's so fat I had to walk three miles to get on her good side.

Do you know the story about the little old woman that lives in a shoe? Your mum's so poor she lives in a flip-flop.

Your mum's so fat that I asked her if she'd tried yoga and she said 'no – let me taste it'.

Your mum's so dirty she tried to take a bath and the water jumped out.

Your mum's so ugly that when she walks into a bank, they turn off the surveillance cameras.

Your mum's so stupid she tried to strangle herself with a cordless phone.

Your mum's so ugly that Dracula banned her from his castle for life.

Your mum's like a DIY store: five pence a screw.

Your mum's so fat she stepped on the scales and they swore.

Your mum's so fat she's got shock absorbers on her toilet seat.

Your mum's so ugly her dentist treats her by mail order.

Your mum's so ugly her pillow cries at night.

Your mum's so foul she got sacked from the sperm bank for drinking on the job.

Your mum's so poor that when I asked her what was she doing in the dustbin, she said, 'Christmas shopping'.

Your mum's so old the fire brigade goes on standby when you light her birthday cake.

Your mum's so poor that her giro bounces.

Your mum's so stupid she leaves correction fluid all over your computer screen.

Your mum's so stupid that in the 'sex' box of a job application, she wrote, 'M, F and sometimes Wednesday'.

Your mum's so fat she's on both sides of the family.

Your mum's so fat that when she walks around in high heels, she strikes oil.

Your mum's so fat we're in her right now.

Your mum's so poor she thinks a 'hot meal' means stolen food.

Your mum's so stupid she spent twenty minutes staring at a juice carton because it said 'concentrate'.

Your mum's so fat she fell off a boat and the captain yelled 'land ahoy'.

Your mum's house is so dirty the cockroaches drive around in dune buggies.

Your mum's so ugly they filmed 'Gorillas in the Mist' in her shower.

Your mum's so ugly your dad takes her to work with him so that he doesn't have to kiss her goodbye.

Your mum's so poor her doormat just says 'wel'.

Your mum's so old

she's got hieroglyphics on her birth certificate.

Your mum's so stupid

she studied for a drug test.

Your mum's so stupid

she threw a rock at the ground and missed.

Your mum's so stupid she sold her car for petrol money.

Your mum's so dirty that when she sweeps the house, the dirt gives her the right of way.

Your mum's glasses are so thick that when she looks at a map, she can see people waving.

Your mum's so fat she doesn't have a doctor, she has a groundskeeper.

Your mum's so fat she's got smaller fat women orbiting around her.

Your mum's so dirty even dogs won't smell her.

Your mum's so dirty she has to creep up on soap.

Your mum's so poor the homeless give her money.

Your mum's so ugly I put tracing paper over her face and drew a gorilla.

Your mum's so ugly it looks like her neck threw up.

Your mum's so ugly that when she entered an ugly contest, they said, 'no professionals'.

Your mum's so fat that when she steps on the scales, they read, 'one at a time, please'.

Your mum's so fat she got hit by a bus and asked who was throwing stones.

Your mum's so hairy Bigfoot took a picture of her.

Your mum's so stupid
that the first time she used a vibrator, she cracked her front teeth.

Your mum's so old
she was a waitress at the Last Supper.

Your mum's so fat I ran around her twice and got lost.

Your mum's so fat she jumped up in the air and got stuck.

Your mum's so fat that when she dances at concerts, the band skips.

Your mum's so ugly that when she sits in the sand on the beach, cats try to bury her.

Your mum's so stupid she went to take the 44 bus and took the 22 twice instead.

Your mum's so stupid she fell up the stairs.

Your mum's so fat that every time she turns around it's her birthday.

Your mum's so poor that when I walked into her house, a cockroach tripped me up and stole my wallet.

Your mum's so fat she whistles bass.

Your mum's so stupid she took a ruler to bed to see how long she slept.

Your mum's so stupid she married your dad.

Your mum's so ugly she has to trick or treat over the phone.

Your mum's so greasy her freckles slipped off.

Your mum's so fat her favourite food is 'seconds'.

Your mum's so fat
I swerved to avoid her on the road and ran out of petrol.

Your mum's so ugly
her passport has a warning label on it.

Your mum's so ugly she
scares wasps away.

Your mum's so fat her stomach gets home fifteen minutes before she does.

Your mum's so old her phone number is 1.

Your mum's so old she's got vultures on her roof.

Your mum's so ugly she practices birth control by leaving the lights on.

Your mum's so fat she wears a watch on each arm – one for each time zone.

Your mum's so fat her belly button doesn't have lint – it has sweaters.

Your mum's so poor that when I go to your house and ask where the bathroom is, she says 'pick a corner'.

Your mum's so ugly even the Elephant Man paid to see her.

Your mum's so fat that when she was born, she gave the hospital stretch marks.

Your mum's so stupid she gets lost every time she blinks.

Your mum's so stupid she asked me what comes after 'X' in the alphabet. I said 'Y'. She said, 'Because I want to know'.

Your mum's like a bowling ball: she gets picked up, thrown in the gutter and then comes back for more.

Your mum's so fat that when your dad climbs on top of her, his ears pop.

Your mum's so dirty that her cleavage looks like it's got an infestation of chicken bones.

Your mum's so fat that when she goes to an all-you-can-eat restaurant, they install speed bumps.

Your mum's so stupid she stands up on empty buses.

Your mum's so old she's older than your grandma is.

Your mum's so ugly her mum had to get drunk to breast-feed her.

Your mum's so fat that she went to the beach and Greenpeace pushed her into the sea.

Your mum's so fat that when Greenpeace had pushed her in, Spain claimed her as a colony.

Your mum's breath is so bad she needs breath mints with batteries in them.

Your mum's so poor that people rob her house for practice.

Your mum's so stupid
she took you to the cinema to see 'Closed on Christmas Day'.

Your mum's so stupid
that when she read on her job application to not write below the dotted line, she wrote, 'OK'.

Your mum's so ugly that her birth certificate was an apology letter from the condom factory.

Your mum's got so much hair on her face she has to braid it into a scarf.

Your mum's so stupid
she puts coins in parking meters and waits for sweets to come out.

Your mum's so stupid
she jumped out the window and went upwards.

Your mum's so fat

that when she steps on chewing gum, she can tell you what flavour it is.

Your mum's so fat

that when she opens the refrigerator, it cries.

Your mum's so ugly

that if ugly was a brick, she'd have her own council estate.

Your mum's so fat

she speaks in stereo.

Your mum heard that opposites attract so she's after someone clever and good-looking.

Your mum's so ugly she looked out the window and got arrested for mooning.

Your mum's like a library: open to the public.

Your mum's so fat she measures 36-24-36 and the other arm is the same.

Your mum's so stupid she got fired from a blowjob.

Your mum's so poor you all go out for Sunday pushes of the skateboard.

Your mum's so ugly that the last time she heard a whistle was when a train hit her.

Your mum's so fat she has to get out of the car to change the radio station.

Your mum's so fat that on Halloween she trick-or-treats two houses at a time.

Your mum's missing so many teeth it looks like her tongue is in jail.

Your mum's so poor that I came over for dinner and she read me recipes.

Your mum's house is so small that I put my key in the front door and broke the back window.

Your mum's so stupid she looks for Sunday papers on Tuesdays.

Your mum's so stupid she got stabbed in a gunfight.

Your mum's so fat that when she went to get an all-over tan the sun burned out.

Your mum's so fat she's been declared a natural habitat for eagles.

Your mum's so ugly

that people hang her picture in their cars so their stereos don't get stolen.

Your mum's so poor

that your family eat cereal with a fork to save milk.

Your mum's so poor that she goes to the fried chicken shop and licks other people's fingers.

Your mum's so fat her shadow weighs two stone.

Your mum's so lazy
she doesn't walk in her sleep –
she hitchhikes.

Your mum's so stupid
it takes her a week to get rid of
a 24-hour virus.

Your mum's so fat
that when she wears a black raincoat, people shout 'Taxi'.

Your mum's so old
she owes Goliath a fiver.

Your mum's so fat
she grazed her knee and gravy came out.

Your mum's so stupid
that when she heard that drinks were on the house, she went and got a ladder.

Your mum's like a bus:
£1.20 a ride.

Your mum's so poor
I saw her busking outside the Job Centre.

Your mum's so ugly that people at the circus pay money not to see her.

Your mum's so fat that they had to change 'one size fits all' to 'one size fits most'.

Your mum's so fat she goes to restaurants, looks at the menu and says, 'okay'.

Your mum's so poor

I saw her wrestling a squirrel for a peanut.

Your mum's so ugly

they put her in a tinted incubator when she was born.

Your mum's so ugly that when I took her to the zoo they thanked me for bringing her back.

Your mum's so fat she uses bowling balls for earrings.

Your mum's so fat

that her kidnappers had to call for backup.

Your mum's so old

her birth certificate says 'expired' on it.

Your mum's so poor

that I asked her what was for dinner and she tried to throw me in the oven.

Your mum's so old

that when she was born, the Dead Sea was just getting sick.

Your mum's so wrinkly she has to screw her hat on.

Your mum's so stupid that I gave her a penny for her thoughts and I got change.

Your mum's like a racing car: she can burn four rubbers in an hour.

Your mum's so fat she has to iron her jeans on the driveway.

Your mum's so fat she's taller lying down.

Your mum's so fat the only pictures you have of her are satellite pictures.

Your mum's so ugly
she makes onions cry.

Your mum's so stupid
that when you asked her if you could get a colour TV, she asked you what colour.

Your mum's so fat
they had to paint a stripe across her back to see if she was walking or rolling.

Your mum's so ugly
the neighbours chipped in for thicker curtains.

Your mum's so stupid she had you.

Your mum's so fat she puts mayonnaise on aspirin.

Your mum's so fat she sat on a lump of coal and made a diamond.

Your mum's so lazy she's got an armrest on her remote control.

Your mum's so fat that she auditioned for a part in 'Indiana Jones' and got the part of the big rolling ball.

Your mum's so ugly she has to tie sausages around her neck to get your dog to play with her.

Your mum's so ugly if you looked up 'ugly' in the dictionary her picture would be next to it.

Your mum's so stupid she tried to insult you and started with 'Your mum's...'

Your mum's so fat her stomach has its own postcode.

Your mum's so fat that when she travels she has to make two trips.

Your mum's got three teeth: one in her mouth and two in her pocket.

Your mum's so poor she waves an ice cream around in summer and calls it air conditioning.

Your mum's so fat they hired her to DJ in the ice cream van.

Your mum's so ugly her shadow ran away from her.

Your mum's so old she left her purse in Noah's Ark.

Your mum's so poor that when I asked what was for dinner, she pulled her shoelaces off and said 'spaghetti'.

Your mum's so fat she got harpooned in the swimming pool.

Your mum's so fat she deep-fries her toothpaste.

Your mum's so fat her belly button's got an echo.

Your mum's so stupid that she goes to 24-hour shops and asks what time they close.

Your mum's so stupid she sent me a fax with a stamp on it.

Your mum's so fat that when you were born, they had to send a search party to find you.

Your mum's so old that when Moses parted the Red Sea, he found her fishing on the other side.

Your mum's teeth are so yellow she walked outside and the sun resigned.

Your mum's so stupid she stepped on a crack and broke her own back.

Your mum's so ugly that when she walks into the kitchen, the rats jump on chairs and start screaming.

Your mum's so poor

I saw her hanging toilet paper out to dry.

Your mum's so poor

that when I saw her kicking a box down the street and asked her what she was doing and she said 'moving'.

Your mum's so fat she masturbates to cookbooks.

Your mum's so old she's blind from the Big Bang.

Your mum's so old she has an autographed Bible.

Your mum's so fat she can't even jump to a conclusion.

All Crombie Jardine books are available from your High Street bookshops, Amazon, Littlehampton Book Services, or Bookpost P.O.Box 29, Douglas, Isle of Man, IM99 1BQ.
tel: 01624 677 237,
email: bookshop@enterprise.net
(Free postage and packing within the UK).

1-905102-50-X

£2.99

1-905102-33-X

£4.99

The Little Book of Wanking

The definitive guide to man's ultimate relief

DICK PALMER

1-905102-00-3

£2.99

1-905102-78-X

£2.99

1-905102-01-1

£2.99

www.crombiejardine.com